Take a Book.   Read a Book.   Return a Book.

Take a Book.   Read a Book.   Return a Book.

HOLLAND

Text and photographs by
Chris Fairclough
General Editor
Henry Pluckrose

Franklin Watts
London   New York   Sydney   Toronto

Words about Holland

Ajax of
   Amsterdam
Alkmaar
Amstelveen
Amsterdam

barges
bulbs

canal
cheese
clogs
crude oil

DAF
Delft
diamonds

Dutch

Edam
Europoort

Friesian cows

Gouda
Guilder

Hague, The
Hall of Knights

Kinderdijk

Marken
Netherlands

oil refineries

Queen Beatrix

Rotterdam
Rubens

St. Nicholas
skating

tulips

Van Gogh

windmills

Zeeland

Franklin Watts Limited
8 Cork Street
London W1

ISBN UK edition: 0 85166 962 X
ISBN US edition: 0 531 04417 3
Library of Congress Catalog Card No:
81-70052

© Franklin Watts Limited 1982

Printed in Great Britain by
E. T. Heron, Essex and London

Maps by Brian and Constance Dear,
and Tony Payne.
The author and publisher would like to
thank the following for kind permission
to reproduce photographs:
Netherlands National Tourist Office
(17, 21, 26, 31); De Porceleyne Fles
(15); DAF Trucks Ltd (18); National
Gallery, London (30).
The author would like to thank Yvonne
Van Balen, Jan Auke and Janneke
Van Werkum for their help.

Holland is a small country in Western Europe. Its proper name is the Kingdom of the Netherlands. The Netherlands means "low lands". The people call themselves Netherlanders. English speaking people usually call them the Dutch.

A city called The Hague is Holland's seat of government. Parliament meets in the Hall of Knights, shown here. Queen Beatrix, opens parliament at a ceremony every September.

Amsterdam is the capital of
Holland and the largest city. It has
many canals crossed by hundreds of
bridges. Some of the houses were
built by rich merchants more than
700 years ago.

Many markets and stalls line the
banks of the canals in Amsterdam.
Flowers are sold all year round in
Holland. Huge greenhouses to the
south of the city produce many flowers.

No cars are allowed in this street. Many towns in Holland have streets where only people on foot or cyclists can go. This shopping street is in Alkmaar, north of Amsterdam.

This picture shows some Dutch stamps and money. The unit of money in Holland is the guilder. There are 100 cents in one guilder.

WORLD
MAP

Netherlands

NORTH SEA

Groningen

NETHERLANDS

Haarlem
Amsterdam

Enschede

The Hague   Utrecht

Rotterdam   Arnhem
Rhine   Nijmegen

Maas   GERMANY

Breda
Tilburg

Eindhoven

BELGIUM

Maastricht

9

The flat country and plentiful supply of water is ideal for dairy farming. This picture shows a herd of Friesian cows grazing on lush pasture in the north of the country.

Much of the milk is used to make cheese. Two well-known cheeses come from the towns of Gouda and Edam. Many shops sell only cheese.

Homes in Holland are clean and tidy. The Dutch like green plants. It is a tradition to leave the curtains open in the evening. Most windows have short net curtains.

Dutch families spend many of their evenings at home. This family lives in a large old house in Middleburg in the south-west. Many of the old buildings here are preserved for their historical value.

The buying and selling of
diamonds is a thriving industry in
Amsterdam. Tourists can watch
men polishing the gemstones. Some
diamonds are very small and just
big enough to make one ring.

Delft is famous for its porcelain china. The best-known factory is called "De Porceleyne Fles". This picture shows the delicate pattern being painted onto a plate.

Children begin school at the age of six in Holland. Many schools are privately owned. The school day begins at 8.30 and continues until about 1.30.

On the 6th of December the Dutch celebrate the birthday of St. Nicholas. He is the patron saint of children. Often someone dressed up as St. Nicholas arrives by barge to hand out presents to the children. It is a day like our Christmas.

This picture shows the production line at DAF trucks. These trucks are known for their good design and strength. There is not a great deal of heavy industry in Holland.

Europoort, near Rotterdam, has some of the largest oil refineries in Europe. Crude oil is brought here by ship and piped or taken by road to many countries in Europe.

During the winter many canals freeze over. People put on warm clothes and skate on the ice. Sometimes they can skate from one town to another along the canals.

Cycling in Holland is popular because the land is so flat. Nearly everybody has a bicycle and many people ride to work or school. The roads have special cycle lanes.

Some Dutch canals are large. Barges carry goods from the towns and villages to all parts of the country. People used to travel by barge, but it is much quicker to go by car because the roads are good.

Rotterdam is Holland's largest
port and second largest city. It is the
busiest port in the world. Many of
the products from West Germany
are exported from Rotterdam.

Windmills are found all over Holland. They were built to pump water from the land into the canals. Some are still in use and people live and work in them. These mills are at Kinderdijk, near Rotterdam.

Nearly half of the land in Holland is below sea level at high tide. Great sea walls have been built to hold back the sea. The seawater has been pumped out. Here a barrier is being built in Zeeland.

Yachting and windsurfing are popular sports in Holland. Many towns and villages near to lakes or the sea have a sailing club where people can learn the sport.

Soccer is played all over the country. People travel great distances to watch their team play. During the winter months the game is played on cinder pitches. The most famous Dutch team is Ajax of Amsterdam.

Some Dutch people still wear clogs which are shoes made from wood. They are waterproof and warm. Here a man is making a pair of clogs in a workshop in Amstelveen.

Some people still wear the traditional costume of their village or town. This lady comes from Marken, near Amsterdam.

Many famous painters were born in
Holland. This painting of Holland
is by Peter Paul Rubens (1577–1640).
Other well known Dutch artists
include Rembrandt and Vincent van
Gogh.

Every spring millions of tulips are grown. They are harvested for the bulbs as well as the beautiful flowers. The other main crops are potatoes, sugar beet and wheat.

Index